The Bestie Code

C. Reneé Mangum
TaVonna Symphony
Emma Sheree

Mangum, Symphony, Sheree

The Bestie Code

Copyright © 2018 The Bestie Code L.P.

ISBN-13: 978-0-692-04019-5

All rights reserved. No part of this publication may be reproduced, distributed, or transmitted in any form or by any means, including photocopying, recording, or other electronic or mechanical methods, without the prior written permission of the publisher, except in the case of brief quotations embodied in critical reviews and certain other noncommercial uses permitted by copyright law. For permission requests, write to the publisher, with the subject line "Attention: Permissions Coordinator," at the email address below.

The Bestie Code Limited Partnership
www.thebestiecode.com

Bulk Ordering Information:
Special discounts are available on quantity purchases by corporations, associations, and others. For details, contact the publisher at the email address above or visit www.thebestiecode.com.

Published 2018 by The Bestie Code L.P.

Edited by The Official Maleeka Group, LLC.

WARNING:

JUST A HEADS UP…

This book contains stories, language and content that is not for the faint of heart. It's all in the name of love, fun, friendship and pure honesty. We are not psychologists, licensed life coaches or anything else that requires certifications to tell you what to do with your life. We're a group of women who have learned through experience what works for us. And we're hoping it'll work for you as well.

You've been warned! Let's do this!

For Janie, Danielle and Shyra

ACKNOWLEDGEMENTS

TaVonna...

To Jaden and Genesis... Jaden, you're my blessing and God knew how much I needed you in my life. Genesis, you're my miracle. I couldn't thank God enough for bringing you into my life.

My two heartbeats. I couldn't imagine a life where you two aren't in it. You two are everything right. Thank you for loving such an imperfect mother. Thank you for understanding the days that Mommy couldn't get out of the bed to play, or the days I had to miss a school event. I fight everyday simply to be your mother. I love you more than every cookie ever baked.

Emma...

I would like to dedicate this book to my three inspirations. Paul Jr., Angel and Gabrielle. Thanks for understanding when Mommy had countless meetings and late nights. Just know that I did this all for you. I am extremely blessed to have you three as my children. I love y'all with all my heart. With God anything is possible and I thank Him everyday for trusting me as your guardian on earth.

Reneé...

My Jays. Hubby Love and Son Love. Everything I do, I do it for you. Thank you for your patience, your support and your love as I pursue my dreams. God has a plan for us, and it's unfolding before our eyes. The possibilities for our little family are endless, as long as we keep Him first.

And to my other besties Star and Nicole, thank you for being there and supporting us throughout this process. All I do is ask and you graciously step in wherever you're needed, without asking for anything in return. The love is so real. You two hold a very special place in my heart.

CONTENTS

	Introduction	i
1	Code 1: Besties Accept Each Other For Who They Really Are	Pg 1
2	Code 2: Besties Push Each Other To Be Great	Pg 16
3	Code 3: Besties Bounce Back	Pg 29
4	Code 4: Besties Set Realistic Time Expectations	Pg 42
5	Code 5: Accepting Your Bestie's Significant Other — The Good, The Bad and The Ugly	Pg 55
6	Code 6: Besties Are Each Other's Checks and Balances	Pg 68
7	Code 7: Besties Build Trust	Pg 79
8	Code 8: Besties vs Everybody	Pg 90
9	Code 9: When A Friendship Just Has To End	Pg 100
10	Code 10: Besties Just Wanna Have Fun	Pg 111
11	You Know You're Besties When…	Pg 130
	About The Authors	Pg 133

Mangum, Symphony, Sheree

INTRODUCTION

This goes out to the everyday woman who longs to have those girlfriends that will be there while you slim your waist, thicken your hair, build an empire, raise your children, find love and live your best life.

This is not a "one size fits all" book. We wouldn't necessarily categorize it as self-help either. Instead, this is a story of how three different women connected in our adult lives and became a bomb ass trio of besties.

What you will get from this book is a raw and honest look into what has helped us build and maintain our very close-knit, tightly woven friendship. You'll read our stories, our perspectives and our life lessons as we vulnerably share with you what we've learned about friendship among women.

We often hear women say, "all of my friendships come from my school days." It seems like such an impossible feat for most women to build genuine, long-lasting friendships with other women beyond their academic years. This especially rings true when we talk to women of color. They meet women all the time; but it never goes beyond the surface. If the friendship goes beneath the surface, it ends abruptly for whatever reason.

This phenomenon amazes us because… well… we've done exactly what we've been told cannot be done. It's not magic. Well, maybe a little bit. But really, the magic is in the lessons we've learned through trial and error. We now refer to these lessons as "The Bestie Code."

As long as we live by "The Bestie Code," we'll be friends forever. Our "Code" has guided us to what is now the healthiest group of friends any of us have ever experienced. We've allowed other ladies to occasionally experience our bond throughout the years, and they've all had the same thing to say about us. Our friendship is all love. Our friendship is healthy. And our friendship works!

As you read this book, keep in mind that friendship is an investment. In the world of finance (and in the diary of Investopedia), investing is defined as "an act of committing money or capital to an endeavor with the expectation of yielding additional profit or income." In terms of building and maintaining healthy friendships, you must be willing to invest every aspect of yourself (your time, your thoughts, your actions, your money and your energy) in an effort to gain a return of an even greater and enhanced version of yourself, as well as a friend who reciprocates what you have invested.

With all investments, there are risks involved. We don't always get what we want from every investment. You have to calculate your risks and use wisdom in deciding when and where to invest yourself. Look at your time, mental capacity and energy as investments. You are not spending time; you are investing time. You can make more money, but you cannot make more time.

Choose your friendships wisely and understand that not all friendships are created equal. Some friendships are meant to be more surface than others, and that is okay.

However, this book is for those who are looking for a way to attract honest, genuine, rooted and grounded girlfriends who will be your best friends, your bridesmaids, your maids of honor, your children's godparents, your hands to hold through tough times in life, your favorite people to do karaoke with on Saturday nights, your ride or dies (although we're not dying anytime soon) and more.

This is a book to deepen friendships you already have, help you build new ones and know when they aren't good for you versus when you're just having a spat. This book will make you laugh, make you cry, give you tips, offer advice, and often make you say, "Yasssss Queen, I know EXACTLY what you mean!"

We've enjoyed writing this book for you and hope you have an even more enjoyable time reading.

Reneé, TaVonna and Emma <3

The Bestie Code

BESTIE CODE 1: BESTIES ACCEPT EACH OTHER FOR WHO THEY REALLY ARE

Acceptance As-Is… Emma's Eyes

So, a rational friend, an indecisive friend and an OCD friend walk into a restaurant…

I know, it sounds like the beginning of a really bad, inappropriate joke. But in all actuality, this is my life.

If you have ever encountered my Besties and I during a breakfast, lunch or dinner date, I would first like to apologize on our behalf, especially if you were ever our waiter or waitress. Ordering food should not be a difficult task, right? But what if one of your friends is OCD when it comes to her food touching? Or what if she was indecisive about her food choices every time, even though she always ends up ordering the same thing? How exhausting could this be for the rational one? These traits could drive anyone mad, but the real question is, would you want your friends to change? As for my crew and I, changing each other is not a part of the plan.

Imagine this:

Waitress: Hello, my name is Jessie! Are you all set to order?

Reneé: I'll have coffee and a Denver omelet. Please substitute the ham for sausage and the regular toast for French toast.

Emma: You know, I'm not sure of what I want… I haven't even looked at the menu. Can you come back to me?

TaVonna: Okay… Listen, sweetheart. I would like one slice of French toast and one egg. Make sure that the egg is dead. Like, dead dead. Absolutely no yoke. Two strips of bacon. And all on separate plates. And bring Reneé a water as well please, no lemon.

I'm sure by now, you've figured out that I'm the indecisive one. Eventually I figure out what I want to eat. Usually it's 20 minutes after the fact, but that is just me.

The beauty of it all is that I don't have to change. Although I try to be considerate of others and have my life figured out ahead of time (at least when it comes to meal choices), I don't always have it all together. My besties accept that.

What does this have to do with successful adult women relationships? Accepting your friends for who they are is critical. If this philosophy is not the foundation of your friendship, you will have a difficult time building a friendship that is genuine.

Friendships at any level take work, but having adult friendships is a different beast. Being a friend is a choice. You can technically walk away at any moment. You do not have to think twice about it. There is no legally binding document making you stay. No one is going to question your decision. With that said, friendships are voluntary commitments that aren't for the faint of heart.

There are many valid and invalid reasons why friendships end. People tend to walk away from friendships because of differences in thoughts, opinions and actions. Some people can accept such differences and others do not know how to cope. Once a woman believes that she is no longer compatible or that her friend is not on her level, she'll dip. I am here to say that if you walk away from every friendship due to your individual differences, then you will never have any friends of real value.

That's why it is important to go into any friendship knowing that the person you met is who they are and will most likely not change, unless they want to. Your outlook has to be that you don't actually want to change them. That's right. To have successful adult friendships, you have to accept your friends and love them for who they are without trying to control or change them. In doing so, your friendships will be a lot easier and, crazy enough, more manageable.

Now, I am in no way saying that if your friend is doing something life threatening such as drugs, that you should accept that behavior. HECK NO! A part of your job as a friend should be to want to help them. What I am saying is that if your friend is a bit snappy all the time, that's just who she is. (You'll meet my snappy friend shortly.) If the two of you have a mutual respect that will not allow her snappiness to go too far beyond your comfort, then accept the facts and keep it moving. It may sound crazy, but believe me, it's possible. I am living proof. Once you learn to accept your friends for who they are, you will then be on the road to a beautiful friendship.

For Reneé, TaVonna and I, our differences and the fact that we don't try to change them is what helped us grow into Besties. Although we are different by nature, our friendship works because we focus more on our friendship and less on what we don't agree with about the other person.

TaVonna is…..Well, TaVonna. Ordering her food is literally a 10-minute conversation. Although it can be very comedic, her filter is non-existent. To the outside person looking in, she may come off a bit strong. And honestly, we've had our fair share of run-ins because of that (I will explain in a later chapter). But overall, I love her more than unicorn stickers and glitter. That may not sound like a lot of love but trust me, it's astronomical!

TaVonna is bossy. She will tell you about your life in 2.2 seconds and think nothing else of it. What's funny is, because I know that is truly her personality, I wouldn't change it. The moment she stops being bossy, I'm sure hell has frozen over and I need to check on my friend. Others may not be able to handle her, but she is who she is, and I love her for that. I often think about what things would look like had Reneé and I decided to try to change her? We would have missed out on a dynamic friend. We would have made her feel uncomfortable around us, possibly to the point of causing stress on herself trying to be someone she's not. Either way, it wouldn't have been an ideal scenario.

Reneé, she is the rational one. She is who I go to for sound advice, whereas TaVonna may advise me to commit murder (again, another chapter). I remember there was a time when Reneé had decided to perfect her walk with God (rational decision, right?). I mean, she completely sold out to the Lord. She was adamant that her life needed a change and that the only way to do it was to dive full speed into her Christian walk.

Now, before I go any further, just know that I am not a heathen. Well, not every day at least. I know the importance of a strong relationship with God. But let's just say, at that moment in Reneé's life, I was not on her level.

During this time of her rededication, it could have been easy for her to judge TaVonna and I and push us to the wayside because we were not in our walk as strongly as she was. But she didn't. She realized that we were who we were, and she loved us no less. She did however start cheating on us with a few new side besties from church, but that's neither here nor there. We will explain side besties in another chapter. The point is, she did not try to change us. She was able to hold true to her walk and yet remain our friend.

I can't stress it enough that accepting each other "as is" is much more beneficial and rewarding than the hassle of trying to change each other. We are able to spend our valuable time building a stronger bond, rather than waste time trying to change each other. We are three very different peas in a pod, slimy and all (inside joke haha)!

Don't Judge a Book…. Reneé's Reasoning

"Never judge a book by its cover." We all know that phrase; yet, so many of us are still guilty of doing exactly that.

One reason I feel some women have a hard time building new female friendships is because they want to be the judge and jury of other women, even before they get to know them. Don't be too quick to write someone off because you think they may not be your cup of tea. Be open to women that are different than you. Just because you're a fashionista and the lady next to you is not, doesn't mean you two couldn't hit it off. You may start by bonding over how crazy you guys' kids are about Minecraft, and eventually discover that you both really love documentaries and scary movies. The next thing you know, you two will be awaiting Halloween together for trick or treating with the kids and then scary movies with the girls. But if you were too caught up in her initial outfit upon meeting her, calling her "Shrek" because she was wearing the shade of green that you despise, you would've missed out on the friendship of a lifetime. Y'all can talk about the green later. Just let the lady show you who she is first.

I've surveyed many women, and the numbers don't lie. They are hesitant to build new friendships with other women because of the fear of being judged. We all claim we don't want people judging us; however, take a moment to examine yourself. Have you passed up on opportunities to get to know certain women at work, at church, at your children's sports events, at karaoke or anywhere else, simply because you don't think she'll be a good fit? Have you avoided knowing certain women because of what someone else told you about them? Are you truly giving other women a chance to get to know you and vice versa before you count them out? If not, guess what… you're judging her. Until you've given yourself time to get genuinely acquainted, you cannot be certain that this woman wouldn't be a great new girlfriend for you.

I'll never forget when I met TaVonna. It was over the phone. I'm a very laid back lady by nature. I'm very friendly yet super chill. When I got on the phone with TaVonna, she was full of personality. I was interviewing her, to determine if she would be a good candidate to join my sorority. As I listened to her answer questions about herself and her level of interest, I paid more attention to her tone than her actual words. I felt that she was very excitable and animated, a very bubbly fast talker with tons of energy to burn. I thought, *my goodness, this girl is happyyyyy*. My opinion of her was not a bad thing at all, but I definitely didn't see us becoming best friends. I figured, anybody with that much energy is going to drive me nuts!

However, once I invited her to pledge with my sorority, she was assigned to be my little sister and I got to know her more. While she is certainly full of personality, we quickly discovered a few striking similarities. One of which was our struggle in conceiving more children. We both had sons that were the same age, husbands nearly the same age and a strong desire to have more children. But it was a struggle. As we watched sister after sister have babies, we had an understanding between the two of us that kept us uplifted, even as we dealt with those feelings of despair in our conception issues.

This unfortunate commonality bonded us more than ever, and it was the beginning of new depth in our friendship.

But what if I steered clear of TaVonna, simply because she was just too dang bubbly for me?! I would've missed out on a friendship that is now one of the best I've ever experienced.

For goodness sake, give other women a chance, even if they do seem to be different at first. Be a fair judge of character, not a superficial judge of first impressions.

Don't meet a woman and immediately start picking her apart.

Don't converse with her to try and figure out all the reasons why you should not be friends.

Be open to listening, understanding and embracing every woman you meet. Even if they don't become your next Bestie, they may become a great movie buddy, group date night friend, foodie friend, mom friend, business associate or some other counterpart that fits within your life.

Be careful not to judge her. Instead, learn who she is and then determine what route to take as far as friendship.

Blunt Friends Lives Matter…. TaVonna's Two Cents

WARNING LABEL: I WILL TELL THE TRUTH, THE WHOLE TRUTH AND NOTHING BUT THE TRUTH.

You know those really mean old folks that people say will live forever? The ones that say whatever in the hell comes first to mind? Well, my Besties are lucky. I'll be around forever to give my unwanted two cents.

Every group of friends has that one friend that you have to love past their faults – even through sickness and health.

I was diagnosed with bone cancer and lupus some years ago. In the beginning, I made a promise to myself that I would try to live as normal of a life as I could, even though I was fighting to live. This state of being became a hard promise to keep. I experienced extreme paralyzing pain on a daily basis. I started to miss birthday parties and holidays. It became harder to keep up with people around me. Throughout my battle with these diseases, I lost friends. They didn't understand just why I missed an event or why I wasn't ever available. They could not understand why my attitude suddenly changed.

I like to think that this experience was the cherry on the top of life's sundae for me. After I beat cancer and got lupus under control for the most part, I had a different outlook on life and a brand new attitude. I decided to live life the way I wanted to and I would be unfiltered and raw.

I have a very strong personality, and like most women, I don't like being told what to do, how to act, or who to be. I am the blunt friend. Now don't confuse being blunt with being mean. I'm just, in so many words, brutally honest. But even in my honesty, I still care about how I treat people.

I don't set out to offend people but I'm sure I do. My patience is thin. I'm always thinking "Just get to the point already!" I'm fine with apologizing when my delivery is harsh. If you can't handle me, don't ask for my opinion. (Oh, but just wait, I'm sure I'll give that to you anyway.)

Life is short and you shouldn't spend it being anyone other than exactly who you are. Those that know you and your heart will accept you for all that you are.

Opposites do attract and sometimes the most unlikely women make the best of friends. The friend who you consider to be the blunt friend may be one of the best friends you've ever had in life. She may push you out of your comfort zone, she's honest (almost too honest), but there's never a dull moment when she is around.

Yeah, I often hear things like this from my girls…

"Did she just say that, out loud?"

"You can't say that."

"She really does mean well."

It's important to embrace each other's differences. Unfortunately, if you're the blunt friend, just know that you may lose a friend or two. And losing them may hurt. This does not mean that you have to be anyone other than your true self. The friends who accept your personality, no matter how bold it may be, are the ones to keep around for a lifetime. Those closest to you know that you have good intentions, and that is all that matters.

BESTIE CODE 2: BESTIES PUSH EACH OTHER TO BE GREAT

Accountability…. TaVonna's Two Cents

I have this best friend. I won't mention her name or anything. But let me just tell you, she's going to be late to her own funeral on purpose. Then, there is this other best friend I have. I'm just going to say that she IS the term, "fashionably late."

Now me, I'm what you call a "planner addict."

I know you're wondering what the hell that is. I can tell you this one thing — you need at least one Bestie that has this addiction. A planner addict may have more than three different planners, and they are all likely being used at the same time. The planner addict will have a sticker collection that would put a 1st grade teacher to shame.

Time is money and in my group of friends, we're all about making money. It is extremely important to have a support system that holds you accountable and pushes you to do better. If your planner Bestie can't send you reminders faster than Facebook can, you might want to take the role of the planner addict yourself.

Reneé is not planner crazy or anything, but a couple years ago I convinced her to get a planner. I upsold the hell out of a $50 planner. She was getting booked to capacity. I explained to her, if she saw it all written down, it would be more effective. In the past, I would keep track of her appointments on iCal but I noticed that pen to paper may have worked a lot better for her.

Side note: Emma was also convinced to get the same planner. Let me just say this… you can't win them all. Love you, Emma

Now, back to Reneé. She purchased the planner and started using it right away. She loved it! Her husband found it to be quite interesting and amusing, because she even embraced the stickers. After some time using the new planner, she realized that she needed something more. Life was getting busier and she needed more space strictly for business. Now, she may not admit it, but I do believe I was her inspiration for her amazing product, "The Strictly Business Planner."

(Insert, "TaVonna was my inspiration" here.)

In all seriousness, Reneé created a tool for something she saw that she and her close friends and business associates needed. I guess I'm not the only friend that specializes in accountability.

Let's face it. Procrastination gets the best of us sometimes. Just because I have a planner for my children, a planner for my business, one for my health, and one to remind my Besties to buy a cake for their child's birthday, doesn't mean that I have it all together. I remind my friends of things and make sure that they are on task with reaching certain goals, and they hold me to the same standard.

You need friends in your life that will motivate you, inspire you, support you, and make sure you never forget how great you are. There is an old saying that goes something like this: Show me your friends and I'll tell you who you are.

"Your self-worth shouldn't be dependent on others, but incredible things are rarely accomplished alone. Friends help." - Jan Johnston Osburn

Encouragement…. Emma's Eyes

According to the New Oxford American Dictionary, encouragement is the action of giving someone support, confidence or hope. This seems like a simple task, right? I mean, encouraging someone doesn't cost anything. It does not cause imminent harm or danger to anyone. It takes up minimal time, right? So, why is it so hard for women, especially those who claim to seek genuine friendships, to practice being encouraging amongst themselves?

When we asked a group of women why friendships between women seems to be few, the lack of encouragement was a primary and repeated reason. If you are not encouraging the women around you, you are missing out on potential lifelong relationships. Encouragement can be an act as simple as saying, "Girl, don't worry. You got this," purchasing whatever item your friend is selling (even if you don't truly need it), or just being present during a special moment in her life.

Now don't get me wrong. I'm not saying that you must attend every event or buy every product. However, you should be the first in line to provide some sort of support, no matter how big or small, even if it's just an explanation of why you can't attend but verbally tell her how truly proud you are and mean it!

As adults, we are told not to care if our family and friends don't support us. We start singing church hymns like, "Encourage Yourself," and start posting memes that say something along the lines of, "As long as I got God, I don't need anyone else."

This may be true to a certain extent, but the real question is, why should things have to be this way? Why should we have to live in a world of solely self-encouragement and a lack of support if we have friends?

Having the title of a friend is not just for decoration, people. It comes with hard work and dedication, just like any other role you have. If you are a mother, manager, CEO or whatever, each role has certain tasks and expectations associated with it. Having the role of a friend, especially a best friend, should not be treated any differently.

It seems that we as women believe that if we encourage other women, we somehow take away something from ourselves. This idea cannot be any further from the truth. If you are truly in a good friendship, the encouragement will be reciprocated. If you are in a lopsided friendship, one that you do not feel is equally balanced, or you feel like you are missing out in this area, you need to have a reciprocation conversation. Providing support, hope and confidence to someone else is non-negotiable in successful friendships.

This isn't a "brag on my Besties" book, but I must take a moment to do just that. Don't take this as me saying that Reneé, TaVonna and I have a perfect friendship, because we have had our riffs. What I will say is that, when it comes to support and encouragement, I wouldn't trade my girls for anything in the world. I can only hope that they feel the same about me.

Over the past four years, I have been on the worst rollercoaster ride of my life. I was in an on-again, off-again marriage. I've contemplated suicide, doubted my self-worth and practically gave up on life. I was in a dark place that I wouldn't wish on my worst enemies. Instead of talking about me behind my back and allowing me to stay in that place, they made sure to lift me out of the dumps. I don't know if you read it or not when I said I was in this space for FOUR YEARS, but that's four Christmases and a leap year that I was leaning on these two for encouragement. They did not complain. They did not leave me. They did not say, "I don't want to hear your problems anymore," although I'm quite sure they've wanted to at times. They have driven long distances and spent countless hours with me, all because I needed a shoulder to cry on. When I was done crying, they would say, "Now get your life together because you are way too smart and talented to be down like this."

They showed me what encouragement is all about.

We've attended BOSS brunches, sat at hospital bedsides and prayed for one another. We've let each other know how beautiful we are without malicious intent, donated to causes that one of us feels strongly about, picked up each other's children from school and more. In some way, shape or form, I know that if I need support from them, I have it and vice versa. Some may think our friendship is a bit extreme, but it works. Without the element of encouragement, it would be impossible.

There's nothing wrong with believing in yourself, but having others support and believe in you makes a world of difference. I hope this encouraged you to encourage your friends.

Jealousy and Friendship Cannot Co-Exist… Reneé's Reasoning

My tagline in my business is, "Just Be Great." I feel that every person on God's green earth has the ability and potential to be great and excel in whatever they want to do. And when you have a few good friends rooting for you on your journey to being great in life, your potential grows and your drive increases.

But there is an ugly, monstrous disease that affects the lives of many. No one wants to ever admit they have it, but we all know it's there. This disease plagues and weakens relationships, especially among women.

This disease is called jealousy. The most common symptoms of jealousy include displaying a constant state of comparison and competition with others, harboring the desire to upstage someone, downplaying someone else's good news, and acting with phony behavior.

If you identify with these symptoms, you may be affected by jealousy. If you identify these symptoms in those around you, understand that you may be friends with someone who is jealous of you.

Hear me clearly. Jealousy and friendship cannot peacefully co-exist.

Jealousy looks different from friendship to friendship. Sometimes, you may find yourself in tough situations while your closest friends seem to be winning at life. Maybe your friends are getting married before you, having children before you, moving into beautiful homes, dating the most charming men on earth, getting promotions at work, or thriving as entrepreneurs. These are situations that can easily incite feelings of jealousy if you are struggling in these areas. If you're the friend that is winning at life, it's possible that your friends could become jealous of you.

If you're wrestling with this ugly issue on either end of the spectrum, all hope is not lost in the friendship. Not all feelings of jealousy are underhanded. And just because someone may be jealous of you, doesn't mean they want to see you fail. There has to be some shifting in the way you think about yourself and/or your friends, in order to push past jealousy and have a healthy friendship.

Many times, jealousy is rooted in insecurity and lack of self-discovery. It's important that you begin to focus your attention on your own journey and purpose in life. The more you begin to understand your purpose and why your journey is the way it is, the less room you'll have to be jealous of someone else's journey. You'll grow a capacity to appreciate another's path and successes while still pursuing your own.

Also keep in mind that, we win some and we lose some. We all need support in both our wins and our losses. For whatever reason, it's easier for some people to show up to your pity parties than to be in attendance at your success parties. If your friend is having a season of celebration, you ought to be the first in line to show them love and let them know how great they are doing. Your friend's success does not serve as a reminder of your failure or shortcomings. Your friends need your positive energy when good things are happening for them.

Don't get caught up in the vicious cycle of comparing yourself to your friends. No one wins in the comparison game because we all fight our own battles and have our own issues.

When it comes to our wins in life, I'm a believer in the concept of a moving life train. Each car on the train of life has a different name on it. Whoever's car is pulled up to the station is the one who is currently unloading blessings. It doesn't mean you don't have any coming. It simply means that your car on the train hasn't yet pulled up to the station. Be patient and know that you'll get your turn. Be happy when your friend's turn arrives as well, even if it's before yours.

If your friend is in a downward spiral in life, you should also be the first one in line to lift her back up and let her know that better days are coming. Be the kind of friend you would want in each moment of life.

Any time those moments of jealousy arise, ask yourself two questions and be honest in the answers.

Why do you want what your friend has instead of what you already have?

Why is your own life not good enough for you?

Whatever the answers may be, the solutions still fall into your own lap. Perhaps you need to be more grateful for your own journey and how far you've come. If your answers reflect that your life isn't the best, it's still not your friend's fault. Your life is your life. Change it if you don't like it.

Overall, if your friend is really your friend, you should be able to be vulnerable with her about your feelings. Sometimes, a conversation will do the trick. If you're feeling inadequate or insecure, put your pride aside and talk to your friend. Give her the opportunity to help or uplift you. She wants you to be great just like you want her to be great.

If you feel like your friend may be jealous of you, remind your friend how amazing she is and how grateful you are that she's with you on your journey in life.

Don't allow jealousy to ruin the magical friendship you two can or do have.

BESTIE CODE 3: BESTIES BOUNCE BACK

Fighting Fair… Reneé's Reasoning

It's almost inevitable that you're going to have those not-so-pleasant moments with your friends. Conflict happens and it's going to test the depth and strength of your friendships.

What I've found is that many women are not as close friends as they want to think they are. If you have the ability to write your friend out of your life as if she never existed because she upset you, you ladies are not really connected.

Some of us are more emotionally driven and provoked easier than others, but we all end up upset with our friend at some point or another. When this happens, you're faced with choices on how to handle the situation. It may be a simple issue that can easily be resolved through conversation over a glass of wine or cup of coffee.

But at times, it may not be as simple. How do you handle it when your friend hits a real pressure point? For me, my biggest pressure points are loyalty and respect. There aren't many things that can make me so upset, that a simple conversation wouldn't suffice. But if I feel betrayed or disrespected, that offense hits a nerve so deeply rooted in my soul that I can't even see straight anymore.

Whatever your pressure points may be, if a friend hits one, you may end up fighting it out. Fights have a way of exposing who a person really is, both positively and negatively. The important thing to remember in this moment is that, the goal is to remain friends. If a fight or disagreement ensues, you have to know how to fight fair.

Emma and I have been friends since 2002 and we didn't have our first fall out until 2015. I didn't even know how to approach it because I had never mentioned Emma's name before with any anger attached to it. With the way I felt, I knew we would have to fight this one out a bit. But I knew that, at the end of the day, this was my friend. I didn't want that to change. So, emotional and all, I had to be careful about handling this conflict.

Emma is different than me. I'm very mellow and it takes a lot to evoke emotion in me, but I still have feelings. Emma, on the other hand, is one of the most emotionally fragile people I know. She wears her heart on her sleeve; whereas mine is typically guarded by iron doors.

Knowing that I wanted our friendship to continue, I had to know how to fight it out with her even though she's very different than I am.

Here are some tips on fighting fair.

Don't assume or make accusations. Your friend may have offended you accidentally. Don't assume they offended you purposely or that they should just know that you're upset. Make it clear that you're mad but in a way that expresses how what they did made you feel. Don't approach them in a, "Why would you do that" manner; instead, approach with, "When you did that, I felt this way about it.."

Do your very best to stay calm. Take a minute, a second, a day, a couple of days or however long you need to calm your emotions before you approach your friend. It's okay to let your friend know that you're upset but not in a mental space that is stable enough emotionally to talk it out yet. Your friend has to respect and understand that, even if it's not what she wants to hear.

When you fight it out, if you feel yourself getting angry to the point of disrespecting your friend, such as calling her names, becoming violent with her, yelling at her, etc. LEAVE. Remove yourself from the situation. Trust me, no good can come from that. Blatant disrespect is not acceptable. Period. This is not reality TV. This is real life. I'm from the east side of Detroit, so I know that women physically fight in real life too. I've honestly been in many physical altercations. However, when someone upsets you, if your mind tells you that you have the right to physically assault them, it's time to grow up sis. It's an immature and unhealthy mindset. Queens don't operate like that. Also, it's not worth the jail time, losing your job, getting sued or a host of other things that could come with losing your temper.

Low blows are a no no. Be careful what you say. If your friend has confided sensitive information in you, this is not your opportunity to use it to hurt her because she hurt you. That's a low blow and it speaks volumes about your character more than anything else. If your friend hits you with a low blow during an argument, her actions present the grounds to question the nature and future of your friendship. No real friend sets out to purposely hurt the other. If this happens, your homegirl may need to go.

Do NOT broadcast your disagreement, especially on social media. Honestly, it just makes you look immature. People who entertain social media drama don't care about the future of your friendship. It's purely entertainment to them. Don't ruin your friendship by airing dirty laundry and embarrassing your friend on social media. And when you talk to people outside of your friendship about your friend, again this reflects negatively on you. It makes you seem untrustworthy to your friend as well as whoever you're talking to. Keep in mind that, even though you're upset, that's still your friend. It may not feel like it in that moment, but you're likely going to get over this. Protect your friend and your friendship, even in the midst of disagreements. That's how good character and integrity work.

Overall, if you have to fight it out, fight fair. That's your girl. Put on your big girl panties and work it out, sis.

Forgive and Forget... Emma's Eyes

I wish I could tell you that having a best friend in your adult life is as easy as counting to 10. But in this day and age, you have a better chance of finding a magical unicorn and riding it into the sunset on top of rainbows than have an easy friendship. I know you're probably thinking to yourself, if it's that hard to maintain a friendship, it's probably not worth it, right? Wrong! The truth of the matter is, conflict is going to happen. Conflict is practically inevitable to avoid but it's how you handle conflict that make the friendship easier to maintain.

There's a phrase that I'm sure you've heard at least once, "forgive and forget."

It's pretty self-explanatory but I'm going to break it down. Does 'forgive and forget' apply if your friend is sleeping with your boyfriend or husband? Absolutely the fuck not! And honestly, if I was your other friend, I would help you hide the bodies. However, if your friend forgot to take the day off for your kid's birthday and couldn't attend the party, does that mean that you write them off? Does it mean you now play tit-for-tat and don't attend their child's party out of revenge? No! You express how you feel, you forgive them and you nip that situation in the bud.

Here's my motto: If whatever happened did not hurt me, my children or someone I truly love physically, then the situation is eligible for forgiveness. And once I decide to forgive my friend, we resume our regular relationship, not some fake, "I barely want to deal with you," friendship.

This also means you don't bring it up later or throw it in your friend's face to re-open the wound or make them feel bad for their prior offense.

Where people go wrong in friendships is when they claim to have forgiven one another but treat each other differently. Why remain so-called "friends" if the relationship is going to be reduced to bald-headed step child status? For a friendship to work beyond an offense, you have to forgive and forget. There is no in between. You can't save the memory and whip it out whenever it's convenient for you, like during future arguments or fights that might happen. Delete it from your memory bank and move on. You have to be black and white about it. Otherwise, your friendship will no longer be genuine. It'll be more like a ticking time bomb ready to go off and destroy whatever foundation you all have left when the next offense happens. You have to pick your battles and decide if not being paid back $50 is worth losing the priceless years and good times you all had together.

I remember a time when TaVonna and I had a falling out. I wish I could give you blow-by-blow details of what happened, but honestly, I forgot. However, all I know is, I texted her with a few choice words that clearly indicated that I was upset. I was not trying to hear anything that she had to say and, at that moment, I honestly wasn't thinking about saving my friendship. I was just that mad. I could tell that she was getting a bit upset as well, but I didn't care. She then finally said, "I'm not having this conversation with you via text, we need to meet up."

All I could think was, "There she goes being bossy again."

However, I agreed with her. We coordinated a time to meet and let's just say, three wine bottles and a box of pizza later, everything was all good. That night, I forgave her and she forgave me. The only time we ever bring up the event is when we laugh about how drunk we were. I obviously forgave and forgot because, as I said, I don't even remember why I was upset.

That goes to show you that it's possible to move past the pettiness. Suppose I didn't forgive her? Suppose we took it further than expected and lines were crossed? Suppose I didn't agree to meet in person and just said forget it? I don't know exactly what would have happened, but I do know I probably would not have had my thoughtful, loving, bossy best friend in my world. And honestly, that's a world I'd never want to live in.

Speak Up… TaVonna's Two Cents

bi·po·lar dis·or·der

noun

1. a mental disorder marked by alternating periods of elation and depression.

TaVonna's definition

bi·po·lar dis·or·der

noun

1. a son of a bitch

I'm the friend that requires a little bit more bounce back and may require it a little more often than others. I was officially diagnosed with bipolar disorder back in college. I had signs of mental illness my entire life. However, in the African American community this is something that isn't always taken seriously so growing up I was just categorized as being "TOO much" or dramatic. There was no bigger Drama Queen than TaVonna.

I've come to the conclusion that human interaction is important – within reason, of course.

Friendships are important, they provide comfort in times of need. But man, oh man, can mental illness can throw a wrench into the situation. When mental illness is involved, situations that seem simple may become stressful because some conditions can have symptoms that can be hard to control. To your friends you may seem confusing, especially if they were just with you and you were laughing and making plans that same night.

A few summers ago I was going through a two-week long episode. I was at an all-time low. My disorder is associated with episodes of mood swings ranging from depressive lows to manic highs. So when I'm up, I'm on Mars and when I'm down, I'm serving water to people in hell.

Throughout the two-week period, I don't think I communicated with either of my best friends. They reached out and I couldn't pull myself together to respond.

What I love about my Besties is they seem to have some "Emergency Plan" when I have these episodes. They don't push me past my limit. They give me space and they let me know that they are always there.

The episode was over and I was back to my normal self, or whatever "normal" is in my case. I attended a sorority meeting and decided to stay longer to watch "Empire." For whatever reason Renee and Emma were not in attendance. Emma just probably forgot.

I had a pretty good night, the meeting was quick and to the point, the show was good, and the wine was even better. After a Facebook post I was asked to meet up for dinner by my two favorite humans.

We went to our spot with the greatest $4 margaritas, I ordered my favorite meal and then these two (the other two authors of this book) ruin it by telling me how upset and hurt they were with yours truly.

In the moment I thought, *well they aren't that supportive,* but after a few sips of my drink I just sat back and heard their concerns. I had hurt their feelings. It had been two weeks and they got nothing out of me and the first day I'm speaking to humans again, I'm somewhere else and didn't call, text, send a bat signal or anything.

I owed them an apology. Not for having a mental illness but for not communicating. This was learned behavior from growing up. If I was having a bad day people would just leave me be until I resurfaced.

If you have a friend with a mental illness, allow me to be their voice for a moment. As the friend with the mental illness, it's important to respect your friend and their feelings. It can be hard to articulate what you need even with the best of friends. It's completely up to you to let your friends into your world. Some friendships will happen organically and some may need a little more effort. You must remember that having good friends means being a good friend. Don't get frustrated or get discouraged as your friend tries to learn the way around your world. Cultivating a friendship a learning experience and it's not always easy.

Thank God for Besties that bounce back. :-)

BESTIE CODE 4: BESTIES SET REALISTIC TIME EXPECTATIONS

The Art of Bestie Day… Emma's Eyes

There are 8,760 hours in a typical year. To most people, this seems like a lot of time! I mean when you think about it, how much can you get accomplished in 8,760 hours? Well, that's 8,760 hours before you take everything else into consideration. The average person needs about 8 hours of sleep a day to be considered well rested. If you're an adult, you typically have a 40-hour work week. So minus 2,920 hours for sleep and 2,080 hours for work; you are left with 3,760 hours to split amongst your family, friends, your alone time and, if you are also building a brand, your business. Eight thousand plus hours may seem like a lot of time, but in reality life can get a bit hectic when you're juggling it all.

Life in general can get busy. It can get overwhelming and just downright stressful. So how do you maintain healthy friendships when you have so much going on in your personal life? I wish I could tell you that it's easy, but it's not. The fact of the matter is; people MAKE time for relationships or people that mean something to them. Whether it's a romantic relationship or your relationship with your besties, making time for others is an important factor.

Does making time necessarily mean spending every waking moment with your best friend? No! Of course not. But it does mean that if you want to build a genuine bond, you have to sculpt out time in your busy life to do so. Investing time into others is a way of saying, "Hey, you are important to me; let me make time for you."

Building successful relationships with other women require lots of communication and understanding. There must be understanding that everyone has a life to live outside of the friendship. One of you may not always be available but the understanding must go both ways.

TaVonna, Reneé and I have always been big on making time for one another, to the point where it might have become a little annoying to our spouses at sometimes. Some of us would argue with our spouse, or in my case (at least this is what he says), it cost me my entire marriage. Apparently our divorce had absolutely nothing to do with his insecurities, mental manipulation or infidelity (insert eye roll here). This is a discussion for another book.

Anyhow, we've always made time for one another. Whether it was a late night rendezvous at Applebee's for happy hour or specifically creating a "Bestie Day" every month to completely dedicate our time to catching up, laughing, joking or hearing our business ventures. The point is, we made time with each other a priority .

I remember when Reneé and I were having one of those weeks. You know, the one when you want to lock yourself in your bedroom, plug your ears and go "lalalalalala"? Yeah one of those weeks. So we decided, let's do a staycation! We planned it, informed the spouses and we dipped. It wasn't an extravagant resort, nor did it take a lot of money. We spent the day in a hot tub in a hotel not too far from our homes. We made time to kick it with one another when we both obviously needed it.

Making time for your friends can be just that simple. It doesn't have to be some long drawn out girl's trip. It can be as simple as a planner decorating session with pizza and wine (yes, we've done these as well), a breakfast date or an invite to go take a dip in the pool. Making time for your friends should be important to you if you truly desire a genuine, long lasting friendship.

We all have our own set of priorities. Yes, we have children. Yes, we have spouses. Yes, some of us have full time jobs and are full time students. But maintaining this friendship is a conscious decision. Therefore, we treat it as an important relationship and, just like anything else in life, you have to put in work, effort and time for it to manifest and grow.

Do we get criticism for our friendship? Absolutely! I don't know how many times I have heard, "You're a grown woman, grow the fuck up.

Grown women don't have besties." Not everyone will agree and others may think it's too much. But ehh…yeah…well, ya know!

Juggling Time… TaVonna's Two Cents

Studies show that moms work an average of ninety-eight hours per week. Ninety-eight hours a week is equivalent to two and a half full time jobs.

Now to those that have children, you're probably nodding your head in agreement. If you don't have children, these numbers seem like a good form of birth control (just saying).

The study of 2,000 American mothers with kids between five and twelve years old found that the average mother "clocks in" at 6:23 a.m. and "clocks out" at 8:31 p.m., for an average work day of fourteen hours.

Four-in-ten moms surveyed said the week felt like a never-ending series of tasks to complete. I laughed at the clock out time. I guess I'm no average mom. Clock out time for me is usually 11:30 pm or so, with a start time of 5:00 am.

This study didn't include being a mom with chronic illness and being married to a man with chronic illness. One who also has a son who is homeschooled and has therapy to help him with ADHD. It doesn't include being supermom to "The Princess of Everything." I know for a fact the study did not include my two Besties that I'm on call for just about twenty-four hours a day.

You would think with such a busy life, having a successful friendship would be out of the question. I'm no Bestie professional or anything, but I do know that having little to no time won't ruin your friendships; however, having unrealistic expectations will.

Keeping a friendship doesn't need to be a huge time commitment, but you do have to make time for what you consider important. Also, remember that your friend who is a mother of three may not have the same time as the mother of one. I can't expect for Emma to drop everything to leave town when she has children she needs to find a sitter for. Reneé can't expect for me to miss a doctor's visit to go grab coffee with her.

It isn't realistic to think that your bestie has all the time in the world just for you. Sometimes, humans set expectations so high that even they can't reach them. I consider my relationship with my best friends to be extremely important and that is why I make sure that I treat them as a priority.

With all that goes on in my life, I can still tell you that my daughter is learning the letter G this week, my son just beat a game I spent too much money on, my husband is taken care of, Reneé has a photo shoot almost every Thursday, and that I have to remind Emma to write a blog post every other day.

What I'm saying is, my life is not lacking. My marriage is secure, my children are happy and healthy. My friendships are flourishing. I'm not choosing one over the other. I am simply making time.

Here are some tips to make sure that you're not nicknamed Houdini or MIA.

1. Text messages are a great way to keep in contact and it requires almost no energy.

2. Use Social Media. Send a shout out to your besties on Facebook, or post old pictures of you all on IG for #throwbackthursday.

3. Show up to planned events. This may require more energy. You may need to contact the bossy bestie to give her a heads up about keeping you on track that day. This may be as simple as reminding you to cook dinner for the kids ahead of time.

4. Come through when it counts. This is going to require the most energy. Go out of your way to attend major events. Show up at 3:00am when they need you most. Drive 45 minutes away. Just show up.

Friendships are give and take, and healthy friendships have appropriate expectations.

1. KTRK. (2018, March 20). Study shows moms work the equivalent of 2.5 full time jobs. Retrieved from http://abc7ny.com/family/study-shows-moms-work-the-equivalent-of-25-full-time-jobs/3239687/?sf185105016=1

So What's The Agreement?... Reneé's Reasoning

Friendships die because of unrealistic expectations. This could encompass so much, but for the sake of this chapter, we're talking about time.

I'm that business-focused friend who believes that there is no such thing as "free time" and that time is not spent, it is invested. Therefore, time is a very precious commodity to me, as I'm sure it is for you as well.

However, I'm also the friend that has my own full-time business and I'm able to set my own hours. I also have a pretty laid back spouse who doesn't mind when I spend time with my friends (within reason, meaning before midnight, but hey, I break the rules sometimes – haha). I also only have one child who is 11 years old, a soon-to-be certified genius who is extremely self-sufficient. So, even though my time isn't free, it's flexible.

I understand that my closest friends do not always have the time availability that I do. And there are days when I am so knee deep in my business that I do not have the time to invest in anyone at all. Does that mean we can't be close friends? Of course not! It means we have to be realistic about what we expect from one another in terms of time.

One of the worst things you can do to your friendship is assume that your friend has the same expectations that you do. I'm that friend that will whip out a friendship contract on your behind, just so you understand exactly where I stand, what I expect, what I will do, what I won't do, how many children I will godparent for you, my spending limit for birthday gifts, my availability for babysitting hours, my "emergency only" hours for calling, etc. Again, I'm about business. And friendship is work.

I speak my expectations so that no one is unclear about what I'm expecting. It's always a breath of fresh air when someone else does the same thing. I won't leave you guessing. I'll tell you straight up that if you text me, chances are I may not text right back because I could be with a client or I could just not feel like it. If that offends you, you would not want to be friends with me. And that's cool. But at least I'm upfront about what I expect and what you can expect from me. It's just easier and takes out the guess work.

Have an actual conversation with your friends about time. What does your friend believe is adequate time for hanging out? Does your friend like to do daytime lunches or late night partying? Does your friend want to take random, spontaneous day trips or take months to plan a great girl's getaway weekend? These questions open up conversations that will allow you to see what the expectations are and see if they are realistic within your scope of life and reality.

Planning ahead is critical when you have friends with very busy lives. As

Emma mentioned, even if you only get to steal one day a month, which we call Bestie Day, then so be it. Plan that day out, make appropriate accommodations and enjoy it to the fullest. Make the most of the limited time you do have by mapping it out.

My best friends also have to be considerate of the fact that I do have more time availability than they do on most days. So there are times when I may do things without them and choose to do it with who they call my "side besties" (insert eye roll here – haha).

I do have other friends who may not be as close to me as my besties are, but they are great ladies who I love to invest time with as well. Some are single, some are married and they each have different time availability. I make time for different friendships based on the reality of their life's complexities. No one friend can get upset that I didn't do a particular activity with her if I know that she is unavailable, since we've already had a conversation about time restraints, obligations and expectations. You see how this works?

Time is one thing we cannot replace in life. Being realistic about the time you have available will help steer your friendships in a healthy and positive direction.

BESTIE CODE 5: ACCEPTING YOUR BESTIE'S SIGNIFICANT OTHER — THE GOOD, THE BAD AND THE UGLY

Be Clear From The Jump... Emma's Eyes

"Friends! How many of us have them? Friends! Ones we can depend on? Friends!"

Alright, I'm not going to spend a whole chapter quoting Whodini lyrics but the question remains. How many of us really do have friends that we can depend on? Better yet, how many of us are married and have significant others? How important are your spouse and friends to you?

If you answered the last question with "very important," there is something you must understand. Just because you have a spouse doesn't mean you should have to give up your friends and vice versa.

There may be scenarios when your spouse is not fond of your friends and your friends may not be fond of your spouse. However, how you set up your boundaries and expectations will determine how smooth your world will run with these two very important but different people in your life.

A perfect world would be everyone getting along and being the best of friends with mutual respect and understanding. But we all know that sometimes that is not the case. Therefore, the importance of friendship should be something communicated to your spouse from the beginning.

During my marriage, I made the mistake of not having that conversation from the beginning. Prior to my marriage, I had friends. Great friends! Friends that had been in my life since grade school. But the moment I got into a relationship, I cut all ties with my friends.

I thought I was doing the right thing by my husband, but I didn't realize I was doing a disservice to both him and myself. By cutting off my friends and not expressing how important they were to me, I had set the unwarranted expectation for my husband to think that he had total control over my social life. He also felt that if he didn't like my friends, I would cut them loose with no problems. When that turned out to be untrue, feelings got hurt, communication became misconstrued and, well, a divorce happened.

Now, please do not take this as me saying that my friends caused my divorce, because they definitely did not. There were many issues within the marriage. But he believed, by me not having this conversation, they were a big cause. All of this possibly could have been avoided if I had set the notion in the beginning that both parties were equally important in my life and that neither one was going anywhere.

Although my first marriage did not work out as planned, I've definitely learned a few things that will help me be successful in my next relationship.

Ladies, if you have friends prior to your relationship, let your man know what it is. Do not give up your friends solely because you got a man. Now, if your friends are on some shady stuff and they are truly not good for you, that's a different story and you handle that situation accordingly. If there is no real reason for your mate to be alarmed, then everyone should be able to at least get along.

Secondly, set out time for your man. Let him know he holds a special place in your heart. Wear that thong he likes out of the blue, plan a date or make that candle light dinner for him. Whatever it is, you have to show him that you want to be in his life as well.

At the end of the day, you can choose who to have and not to have in your life. No one should have the option to dismiss the other. They don't have to like it or love it, but they do have to respect it.

Mr. Asshole of the Year… TaVonna's Two Cents

I hate my best friend's husband.

Wait!

Okay, let me start over.

My mother always told me that if I didn't have anything nice to say, then shut the hell up. Now I know there may have been a nicer way to say that, but I guess it would've had to come from a nicer mother.

Moving on…

So there's this guy that's in your best friend's life. He's not Mr. Absolutely Right. He is not even Mr. Almost Right. He's Mr. Asshole of the

Year.

But for some reason he exists and you have to learn to co-exist. It doesn't matter if you were there first or if he was there first. There happens to be a very important common dominator — Your bestie. She loves him and it looks like there is no light at the end of the tunnel. He isn't going anywhere and neither are you.

The word of the day, my friend, is cordial.

cor ·dial

ˈkôrjəl/

adjective

1.

warm and friendly.

"the atmosphere was cordial and relaxed"

Let's go over a few examples.

Let's say you want to throw your bestie a birthday party. You want all of her loved ones there to help celebrate. You can't forget to coordinate schedules and details with the human she married. The not-so-friendly thing would be not inviting him, but you're practicing being cordial. So you're going to invite him and make sure he's in on the planning.

Next example. The universe keeps putting you in the same space as this human for some ungodly reason. You walk into a room full of people and, of course, you speak. Naturally you head to sit by your bestie and you-know-who is next to her. Say a simple, "Hello (insert slight smile here), how are you?" And there you have it. You were a mature cordial adult.

Okay, seriously, listen up. He's not your best friend and hell, you may not be his favorite person in the world. He may be rude, a bit of an asshole to your friend, but think about how your dislike for him and his for you affects your friend. Remember that this can be painful and hard to navigate in one's life. In your friend's mind, both her spouse and bestie have major roles.

Along with being cordial, why don't you try a few of these tips to help your bestie out?

- Be honest.

There is a time and place for everything and lucky for you, there is a time when you can speak up about your bestie's mate. Be sure to check yourself and make sure it is coming from a place of concern. If there are signs of abuse, whether it be physical, verbal, or mental, you need to speak up. Have tough conversations with your friend when needed. If you saw him out with someone who looked nothing like your bestie, say something.

- Learn when to stay quiet.

Your feelings about your friend's spouse are not going to change the way she feels nor should you want it to. Let's say that he's an okay guy and you just don't like him for whatever reason. You might want to just keep your emotions to yourself. Staying quiet may help the friendship.

- Don't judge a book by its cover.

This could be a toss-up, because people change. Right? Maybe in the past he was a horrible guy and left a bad taste in your mouth. Maybe Iyanla fixed his life and he feels that he deserves a chance to be looked at in a different light. Your bestie seems convinced and it seems like you'll both be around for a long time. So stop looking for the bad in the guy and work on not judging him.

Boundaries, Get Some… Reneé's Reasoning

A part of being a good friend is knowing how to respect your girl's boundaries. But ladies, in order for your friends to respect your boundaries, you have to set some. Let's talk relationship boundaries.

Boundaries are in place to safeguard something you love. It's not a way of saying, "I don't trust anyone around this." Boundaries say, "I love this thing so much, I have to protect it."

Single ladies, if your friend sets boundaries in regards to her significant other, don't take it personally. It's not necessarily because she thinks you're after her man. It's not about you as much as it is about the principle of respect.

Taken ladies, don't assume that your boundaries are the same as your friend's boundaries. What you may deem as appropriate, she may not. Communicate your boundaries. Respect yours and your friends' boundaries at all times.

For example, let's pretend that your friend is hosting an event at her home and her husband will be there. She comes to you and says, "Now listen, don't come over in those little booty shorts you like to wear." Is she attacking you and your style? No. Is she throwing shade? No. Does she think you want her man? Probably not. Is she setting a boundary for what is appropriate and inappropriate in her home or around her husband? Yes.

Respect it. It's her home. He's her man.

Another example. Let's say that you and your friend are in the midst of a conversation on the phone and her man comes home. She says, "Hey girl, Jay just got home. Let me call you later or tomorrow." Is she disregarding your feelings or conversation? No. Is she being manipulated and controlled by her significant other? Probably not. Is she setting a boundary to safeguard the time she has with her man? Yep. Respect it. That's how relationships stay strong. Don't get upset. She still loves you. But she has to also make time for her relationship.

Just like clear expectations, boundaries allow the people in your life to understand how you operate and teaches them how to respect and treat you. Just like it's important to let your significant other know what your friends mean to you, you also need to let your friends know that your relationship is very important to you as well.

By setting boundaries around your relationship, you are also sending a message to your love interest that they hold their own sacred space in your world. Make sure you let your significant other know that you value your relationship in a special way that is completely separate than that of your friendships. Don't assume he knows, tell him.

Many times, my husband has felt like I put my friends before him. That shook me. How could he feel like that, even though my friends understood that he was my top priority? I discovered that I had let my friends know my boundaries for my marriage and my household. But I had never communicated those boundaries to him, to let him know how important he is to me as well.

He didn't realize that every time I heard him arriving home from work, I would get off the phone with my friends so that I could devote my attention to him. He didn't see all the hang out opportunities I turned down on Friday nights just so that I could sit on the couch with him and watch movies. He had no idea that I have told my friends early on, "I don't play about mine. Don't try me."

No wonder he was becoming resentful of my friendships at times. I had to show him his importance by not only communicating my boundaries to my friends, but to him as well.

Your marriage should be your first priority. My girls mean so much to me, but there is a hierarchy that they understand and respect. If hubby needs me, hubby gets me first. And since he understands that I live by that principle, he also respects my friendships and how much they mean to me.

Decide what respect looks like for you. Communicate those boundaries to your friends and your significant other. But do understand that you should not have to isolate yourself to only your man or only your friends. There should be a healthy balance and both sides of the balance should be respectful and respected.

BESTIE CODE 6: BESTIES ARE EACH OTHER'S CHECKS AND BALANCES

Call The Fixer... TaVonna's Two Cents

I've been known to need either Olivia Pope or Annalise Keating when I'm angry. I have what you would call anger management issues. I'm not a "count to ten" kind of girl.

I mean, I don't know why some humans are just so stupid. Or why they exist, for that matter. It's a good thing that I have friends that do weekly checks and balances with me. Because..truth be told: We are all out of bail money. Lol!

While I may be the friend that requires a little bit more balancing, I find that having a friend like me is both a blessing and a curse. When you have a friend like me, you know that if anything happens to you, someone is going to pay. If someone makes you cry, they're going to have to answer to your "how to get away with murder" friend. I own it!

Let me clear the air and let you know that I did not get this way overnight. Something or someone usually happens to make someone feel the need to defend and protect. And just like the next person, I too have a story.

Almost nine years ago, I decided to marry this human being. Don't worry girl, he's still a living breathing human. I didn't kill him back then. But I will say, at least 1,678,345 times, he was almost thrown off a balcony.

I can't remember if it was my 6th or 7th wedding anniversary, but the human I married failed to plan something to celebrate. Now, in his defense he sucks at planning a trip to the damn bathroom. So, I don't know what I expected.

I walk in the house and he's in bed chilling. I look around and there's not a lily, a rose, or a snickers bar in sight. I go into the bedroom to have a conversation about his lack of initiative. Here's the conversation.

Me: Hey, what's the plan tonight?

I was so angry. I was in tears. Hell, I was on my way to see Judge Lynn Toler on Divorce Court.

I left the house to spare his life and to calm down. I called Reneé and told her the story. I call her often to make sure I'm not just tripping. She's the rational one, so she doesn't always say what I want to hear. But I know whatever she says is for my own good so I listen.

She listened and acknowledge how upset I was. After she told me how wrong he was, of course she had to be her rational self. She just has to play devil's advocate.

Rational Reneé: Well you all should take turns planning these things.

Throw Him Over the Balcony TaVonna: Well, I planned last year.

Rational Reneé: Go talk to him and tell him how he made you feel.

Throw Him Over the Balcony TaVonna: *rolls eyes* I'm about to hang up.

Rational Reneé: Okay, well after you hang up, go plan something for next year.

Being able to keep checks and balances with your friends is extremely important. You should never have a problem communicating with one another. Friendships should be all about making one another better and building each other up.

Call Me T.T.... Emma's Eyes

Who remembers the movie *Set It Off*? Do you remember how the four women had a relationship that many may not have understood, yet they were each a perfect piece to a larger puzzle? The task that they had required them to be each other's conscience, so to speak. Frankie was the loud mouth, Cleo was the hot head, Stony was the level-headed one and T.T. was the emotional one. Somehow they all meshed, but most importantly, they balanced each other out. How many times did Cleo want to kill someone on sight? However, she had the other three in her ear reminding her of the consequences. How about the part where T.T.'s baby drank cleaning solution and almost died? Her friends were there to keep her emotions in check. Now granted, your group of friends may not be bank robbers (at least I hope not), but the elements of their friendship should exist in all friendships today to be successful.

The key word here is balance. Being best friends mean that more often than not, you might have the job of coaching your best friend not to jump off a cliff, when all she can think about is ending it all. Or, although you would help hide the body, you may need to advise her not to commit murder. We've all been there. At least my Besties and I have. Life has its way of throwing curveballs and sometimes we all tend to lose a little bit of our minds. It helps to have that one friend, or in my case two, that says, "Girl, he's not worth the jail time," or, "Think about who you're leaving behind if you hurt yourself."

I'm not saying that you as the friend should assume all responsibility for your friend's emotions. What I am saying is, it may be a part of the job description to be a part of your friend's checks and balances system.

Out of the three of us, I am definitely the emotional one. I wear my heart on my sleeve and I get stressed out about different things all the time.

I've stated before how I would contemplate suicide and my friends would have to remind me how that is not a smart decision.

Checks and balances requires you to not to be the "yes" friend. Not everything and every situation is going to allow you to agree with it her. Sometimes, your friend is going to need you to use your stern but respectful tone. What if my friends were the type to say, "Oh, you want to kill yourself? So do I!" First of all, that would have made me feel like crap. And secondly, the situation probably would have ended badly.

The balance should be well-rounded and everyone should participate. As the emotional friend, I can be that soft understanding ear that my friends may need.

For example, TaVonna has wanted to throw her husband off the third floor balcony ever since I've known her. The funny part is, I don't think she was ever kidding. In fact, I know there were days she was not kidding. Reneé, being the voice of reason, and myself, having a soft heart for everything living, were able to give her the balance she needed to not end up behind bars right now. I personally think her husband should thank God that we're in her life. Lol! Just kidding… or not?!

At the end of the day, don't be afraid to check your friend because she may need you to balance her out.

Just Call Me… Reneé's Reasoning

There's a time for everything. A time to laugh, a time to cry, a time to talk, and a time to listen. It's the balancing act of life. Let's be honest though. Sometimes, when we are faced with a time to stop and think, many of us move and react. In the heat of life's moments, some of us are quick to handle things without really thinking it through. Having your friends around to balance you out in those tough moments can help, if your friend is going to actually help and not make the situation worse.

Within my Bestie circle, I'm the rational one. I'm the friend that will patiently talk you down off the edge and help you see things from a different perspective, without matching your level of emotion. Pay attention to the last part though of that sentence. That's the key to it all.

You need a friend that will be with you through your tough moments without amplifying the way you feel. Instead, this friend will look for solid solutions to problems, remind you to think when you're not thinking and speak wisdom in situations that don't seem to be going your way.

I'll admit, it's not always easy. When someone upsets TaVonna and she wants to throw them from a balcony, it's tempting to say, "You grab the head, I'll grab the feet."

When someone makes Emma cry, it's tempting to just console her and then run whoever it is over with my car.

But I know that's not what either of them need in those moments. Someone needs to be level-headed and sound in their judgment. That someone is usually me.

Here's the tricky part of being the rational friend. Sometimes, your other friends can feel like you don't care that they are upset or sad. They may get the feeling that you're insensitive or not being compassionate. The reality is quite the opposite. If you're in the position of being that friend, you are loving your friend enough to decline her invitation to her pity party and not allowing her to go either. Understand that you have a responsibility to tell your friend the truth, help her thrive and grow and show her better ways to deal. It is not your duty to coddle her fears, woes, insecurities, weaknesses, anger or sadness. Don't enable your friend's feelings in these moments. Bring her out of the dark hole with logical reasoning.

Fair warning. She is NOT going to want to hear your reasoning and rational thinking. She wants to go to her pity party and she wants you to come along for the fun! She might be upset with you at first, because you didn't give her the response she may have wanted. However, the best thing you can do for your friend is to be gentle yet rational with her, not match her level of intensity or pity. Compassion comes in many forms. It just won't come in the way she may want it at the time. Allow your compassion for your friend to spring you into action in sound and rational ways. Your friend isn't thinking in her turmoil. Be her brain. Guide her and motivate her to do the right things. Remind her that you love her, and that's why you won't let her roll around in her sorrow or dive off the deep end into a pool of anger. Be her balance in hard times. She'll thank you later.

BESTIE CODE 7: BESTIES BUILD TRUST

Vulnerability.... TaVonna's Two Cents

Going out, taking road trips, and making memories to laugh at for years to come are some of the greatest benefits that friendships offer. Participating in relationship building activities help you express who you are in a way that lets others know that they can trust you.

Vulnerability is often seen as a weakness and for most women, being vulnerable in any relationship can be a challenge. It's scary to expose your true self and allow people to see you for exactly who you are. Embracing your vulnerability instead of avoiding it can help you have authentic friendships.

What if staying and being vulnerable with those safe people in your life ruins your plan? It's okay. Everything comes at a cost.

Friendships are an investment and vulnerability is a large check to cash. I'm not only talking about being able to share whatever you write in your diary. But being able to expose fears out loud and in living color. Letting a friend "in" can mean that they can hurt you more because of this new important role they play in your life.

Most of the time, vulnerability in any relationship will happen when you're apologizing, trying to explain our actions or trying to help them understand why you reacted in a certain way. Vulnerability creates accountability and that's a huge responsibility to bear.

I have an anxiety disorder that is managed by medication; it's a pain sometimes. I used to find myself making excuses about why I couldn't do something or why I can't show up. For me, I felt that my panic attacks should be something I was ashamed of. That's what I made myself believe. It may sound silly but goodness, I have anxiety about everyday life.

This is going to sound even crazier but for some strange reason, when I order breakfast, I ask for everything to be put on separate plates. It drives me mad when I see bacon, eggs, hash browns and my French toast on the same plate. My Besties totally thought it was unbelievable, but after a while they realized that this was something that I needed to do, even though they have to explain to others why on earth I need four or five plates.

It became so much easier to just open up about the disorder I had rather than to miss out on future outings. When I made the decision to show my authentic self, it opened up a world that allowed me to experience a true connection with my friends.

Vulnerability is not a weakness, but it does take practice and patience. We can all agree that it's not wise to be vulnerable with just anyone. It is important to allow yourself to be vulnerable with the right friends. This act should only be done with what I call "safe humans." Not Brittany from the 3rd grade. You told her you liked the most popular boy and by lunch everyone knew. Not everyone is safe. The "safe human" isn't judgmental. She believes that you're not your mistakes. She doesn't mind the fact that when you order your food, it's more like a lecture for the server. Remember these things when you're attempting to be vulnerable:

- It's okay to let your guard down.

- It's very human to feel.

- Take the risk.

- Most importantly, you'll learn who your real friends are.

I have two Besties that I know without a doubt will take my secrets to their graves. When I call them in distress, they are in the car before I can hang up the phone. I've allowed myself to be completely open with my Besties. With them, I let down all my walls. I share my fears. I don't have to be strong all the time, because I know that they will be there to help me when I'm weak. All worthwhile relationships should allow space for vulnerability.

I Tried To Be Her Friend.... Reneé's Reasoning

A part of building trust in a friendship is learning and knowing who you are dealing and why you are dealing with them. Most of us been burned by someone we trusted. Those experiences teach us how to caution ourselves when trusting others. However, just because Ashley screwed you over doesn't mean Brittney will too. If you want to build new relationships, you can't penalize your new friends for the sins of the old friends.

I met a young lady some years back. We started building a rapport in college because we were in similar life situations. After college, we reconnected as adults and she expressed how much she wanted to build an actual friendship with me.

In attempting to do just that, I would go out of my way to spend time with her, get to know her, allow her to get to know me, introduce her to my friends, set up play dates for our kids, introduce our spouses, and more. But it seemed like, not only did she not trust me, but it was almost as if she didn't want to. I was perplexed by that. I remember thinking, *If you don't even want to try and trust me, how can we ever be friends the way you desire to be friends?*

I would invite her to go places with me, but she never seemed to be available. Our communication was primarily via phone since her time was so limited, due to family obligations. Eventually, I started learning her patterns of availability. So, if I wanted to go somewhere when she was unavailable, I wouldn't put her through another situation of having to tell me no. I simply didn't invite her since I knew she wouldn't be free. But low and behold, she was upset with me because she didn't get invited. Not only was she upset, but she started saying that I was a "fake friend" because of it. She called herself blasting me on social media and everything. I was so confused.

When I told her my logic behind why I didn't invite her and how that shouldn't change the dynamic of our growing friendship, she opened up to me. She said, "I'm sorry. I've always wanted a friend like you – one who actually cares about me. But I don't know how to even receive it. All of my old friends were fake."

Her story let me know two things: one, this young lady has probably never had a healthy friendship in her life; and two, I was going to have to pay for all the mistakes her former "friends" made if I was going to build something with her.

I was already exhausted and over it. But being who I am, I gave her the benefit of the doubt, and I continued to try and grow a friendship with her. But time and time again, she would accuse me of being "fake" any time I didn't do something with her, didn't invite her somewhere, didn't tell her all of my business, or made a new friend. Enough was enough.

I had to stop pursuing that friendship. And while I do hope that she grew beyond the hurt from her former friends, I had to make a choice. My choice was not to be abused or to be in a one-sided friendship. I was not out to get her, and I refused to be treated as if I was.

If you want to build new friendships with women, you cannot assume that they will be just like everyone else that has hurt you. If that's your immediate assumption, then you, my dear, are not equipped to build new friendships.

If all of your friendships end terribly, everyone else may not be the problem – you may be. Sis, you probably have some inner healing that needs to take place. Otherwise, you will continue to be the reason that your friendships do not last. You could miss out on some amazing, lifelong friends by having a victimized mentality.

If you have healthy perspective about yourself and have dealt with the issues of your past, give new people an opportunity to show you who they really are. Use caution but don't be so quick to think that no one can be a legit friend to you just because you ran into a few mean girls before. If those mean girls were back in middle school and high school, it's time to move on and get over it. You were children. Whatever they did was dumb and immature. Don't let that hinder you from experiencing life with new and potentially great girlfriends.

Don't Let Mean Girls Ruin You.... Emma's Eyes

Mean girls, believe it or not, truly exist. Mean girls are the girls who were most popular in grade school, who never wanted to be seen with the nerdy, unpopular girls. These girls are now adult women who have nothing positive to say about other women and who likes to pretend that other women are less than them to make themselves feel better. Even as adults, they exist. And with the help of social media, it has become easier for these venomous snakes to propel their hatred onto others.

Living in a world full of catty women can make it tough to trust anyone, let alone another woman. But honestly, you can't project the bad experiences you've have had with one woman on to another.

Sadly, it happens more often than not. A woman gets bullied and the next thing you know, she shuts down and ostracizes herself from those who may genuinely want to be her friend.

I was once that girl. I've always been a laid back, smart chick. When I was younger, those were not the qualifications that were good enough to be accepted amongst my peers. I was also dark-skinned and chunky. My parents weren't wealthy and I had a gap between my two front teeth that stretched from here to Mexico. I was often singled out because I didn't look like the other girls. Children can be so cruel.

I vaguely remember in middle school, all of the popular girls started a group similar to what some would see as a sorority. They gave each other nicknames and had matching shirts. It was pretty cool, at least at that time (but now that I think about it, those girls were dumb). My best friend at the time, who shall remain nameless, wanted to be a part of that group. She had the potential of being a cool girl; whereas, I wasn't even close to fitting the description. The mean girls pretty much gave my best friend an ultimatum. Either she would continue sitting at my lunch table or be a part of their clique. She decided on the latter. Although it only lasted for about two weeks before she wanted to be friends with me again, her decision let me know where her loyalty was and it wasn't with me.

I never really spoke of the situation but I was truly hurt. Those little evil whores had each other and wanted to take the only real female friend that I had at the time. And they succeeded.

My point of that little story is, suppose I let the disloyalty of that one friend dictate the way that I interacted with any other girl or woman that I had come across? I wouldn't have the friendships that I have today, that's for sure.

I'm not saying that it didn't have any effect on me at all, because it absolutely did. I was the girl in high school who wore hoodies and baggie jeans all the time, just so that I wouldn't be noticed. Then, in high school Reneé came along and wanted to be my friend. I questioned sometimes why I became her friend because the girl was nuts! But she was genuinely my friend. I allowed a new Bestie to get close to me regardless of the bad past experience. I'm absolutely glad that I did because I gained a Bestie for life.

So as the friend who may be projecting your past hurts onto others, stop and ask yourself, *why*? Has the individual really proved to be unworthy of your friendship or is there some underlying hurt or pain you have? If so, talk about it. Your friend may be able to reassure you that, her friendship is genuine and stabbing you in the back is not in her plans. Who knows, maybe you all can then create a Mean Girls club of your own because as for my Besties and I, "You can't sit with us!"

Just kidding!

BESTIE CODE 8: BESTIES VS EVERYBODY

Don't Be Like Kim.... Reneé's Reasoning

This is Kim.

Kim and Ashley are besties.

Kim had a conversation with Kisha and Kisha was talking mad trash about Ashley.

Kim said nothing and let Kisha talk.

Kim is now suspect and is not to be trusted.

Don't be like Kim.

Let me tell you something.

If you have a problem with my Bestie and you want to say something negative about her, do not say it to me and do not let me overhear you saying it to someone else. And if you consider yourself my friend and you tell me that someone said something foul about me, my first thought and question will be, "…and what did you say?"

Furthermore, if someone said something foul about me directly to you, not only am I wondering what you said in return, I'm also wondering why that person felt comfortable talking to you about me. They must've known you wouldn't defend me.

It drives me absolutely insane when I watch something on TV and I witness this kind of friend-on-friend crime like in the example above. Newsflash Ashley, Kim is not your friend, girl. She is suspect and is not to be trusted.

Friends do not allow others to disrespect you in your absence. No one should feel comfortable talking negatively to your friends about you. And no one should feel comfortable talking negatively to you about your friends. That is completely unethical and unacceptable in the code of Bestie Law.

What happened to the days of defending your friend's honor? This should be expected and reciprocated in any friendship. If you hear untrue or unflattering remarks being said about your friend, you should have your friend's back and shut it down. You don't have to be disrespectful or end up in a fist fight because someone said something about your friend. However, there is nothing wrong with saying, "Hey, that's my girl and you're not going to talk about her, especially when she's not here to defend herself." That would be my response in order to keep the peace on a good day. On a not-so-good day, I may say a bit more and tell you a few things about yourself.

Either way, speaking up is better than allowing the conversation to happen and not saying anything. No one likes to create or be a part of drama (well, at least that's what most people claim). However, silence can be easily misconstrued as your agreement with and/or entertainment of the comment.

When those moments happen that you have to check somebody about your bestie, I believe you should let her know. Not in an effort to further irritate the situation, but so that she has an understanding of what is being said about her and from what sources.

There's no worst feeling in friendship than finding out that someone threw shade at you in the presence of your best friend and she said nothing, or worse, entertained the conversation. It demolishes any trust you may have had in that friendship. If this happens to you, talk to your friend. Ask her what happened. Confront this issue right away and then decide if this is truly your friend or not.

Defending your friend's honor shows your loyalty, integrity and respect for your friendship. It also keeps the people honest around you when you silence people's gossip. If you can't trust your girl to step up for you when you can't step up for yourself, that's an issue.

This Time, You Really Can't Sit With Us.... TaVonna's Two Cents

If both my Besties walk into a room, please believe there is an invisible place card that sits us right next to each other. No questions asked. And it's not up for debate.

This isn't a page from the script of Mean Girls, but there really are times where you can't sit with us. Going to a wedding, networking or special event without your girls makes you miss something. You don't feel complete without your girls. I don't know about you but at least one of my besties have to be next to me to pinch me when I'm being too mean or whisper to me to fix my face. Hey, it is what it is and I welcome it.

Ladies, you know you have to be right next to your bestie when you all are in the same room. I mean, the event just won't be enjoyable any other way.

You have your friends and then you have your really good friends. But then, there are certain friends that you practically shared a womb with in some past life. They are your partners in crime, your besties. Having best friends is awesomly crazy but can also be an enabling mechanism. Some may think that you and your girls are weird and even say that you all are too close. Forget that noise. It's besties versus everybody.

In all fun, sometimes the moment only calls for you and your besties. When you're having problems in your marriage, when you need to share something personal, or when you accidentally throw someone over a balcony, your besties are your "go-to" squad. I don't need someone I didn't vet as an accessory to my crime. Besties are the most reliable to keep every dirty detail about your life.

Okay, I digress.

Sometimes, it's just too exhausting trying to bring an outsider up to speed. There are just things that only your best friends would understand. You have inside jokes and stories. Finishing each other's sentences comes naturally. You can look at one another and know exactly what the other one is thinking. You find yourself saying the same thing at the same time. You all practically have your own language (you can even decode random grunts).

True friendship is something to value. This kind of relationship doesn't just go away. At the end of the day, you all understand the commitment of the partnership. Yes, you're protective of them mentally and physically. You always want the best and they want the same for you. There's an invisible shield that is put up around you. Through thick and thin, you have to be a consistent friend and will always stand by them, no matter what happens. There's nothing quite like having someone around who totally understands you and won't judge you.

It's Not A Game.... Emma's Eyes

"It's green and it lives outside!"

"A praying mantis!"

"Correct!"

"It's an animal!"

"A Giraffe!"

"Yes!"

What you have just read are actual commentaries from a game of Taboo with my Besties and I being on teams. We can literally use the most generic clues and nine times out of ten, the other two will get the answer correct. During the time when we all participated in married couples game nights, we reigned supreme against our spouses. They were always questioning our special best friend powers.

Now you may be wondering what on God's green earth does playing a game have to do with having a successful female adult friendship? Everything.

Although having the emotional, moral and physical support is important, having a bestie on the same competitive level as you is crucial during those random game nights. You can't be my bestie if during said game nights, you are as bright as a wet match in a dark cave. You can't be my bestie if during a game of spades, you say you can make 12 books, but your hand is so red, it's practically bleeding. Okay kidding, you can be my friend. However, just know that if I give a clue that the object is round, damnit you better yell out "Pluto" and be correct. It's just common sense!

Best friends usually have a special bond that no one else understands. At times, people will get angry, talk crap about your friendship and even try to throw shade. At the end of the day, it's besties vs. everybody, even in a friendly game of Taboo.

When you are best friends with other women, there is an underlying rule that if there's a reunion happening and your besties are in attendance, you're automatically roommates. If Tank personally gives you four tickets to his concert, no one should fix their lips to ask who you're taking. Well, maybe there is an exception for the last example, if and only if your best friend absolutely cannot make it. Otherwise, there should already be a ticket placed to the side for her (This really happened by the way. Thanks Reneé!). And if there is an idea to write a book for women called "The Bestie

Code," guess who the two other authors are?

I'm not insinuating that your best friend should become your secret lover or anything. But if you are truly best friends, there are just some things that should not have to be questioned, explained or contemplated.

BESTIE CODE 9: WHEN A FRIENDSHIP JUST HAS TO END

We Need to Talk.... Reneé's Reasoning

I'm all for different levels of friendship. You have your besties, who are closest to you. You have your friends who are more of casual and social acquaintances. You have your work friends that are super cool to have lunch with and goof around at work, but that's as far as it goes. And then you have your friends by association, the ones that you only really hang out with because of mutual friends.

Most of these friendships are usually more on the surface and can fade easily from your life without much consequence. They tend to be seasonal and, when they end, it's amicable with no love lost.

Friends are the best, until they become the worst. Unfortunately, we do have those occasional situations when you consider ending a friendship with someone who has left a lasting impression. There are tons of guides that help you deal with ending romantic relationships. But what about those circumstances when you considering ending a really close friendship?

Of course friendships are not legally binding, but let's be honest. Some of y'all are closer to your friends than you are to your spouse. If the friendship comes to an end, how will you deal with that?

First of all, as you've seen throughout this book, we are all about working through the bumps in the road and maintaining friendships. However, we advocate for maintaining healthy friendships. If you're noticing that some of your friendships may be toxic, it's okay to end them.

If your friend is bullying you, pressuring you to partake in behavior that is unbecoming for you, making immoral requests of you, putting your life or health at risk, putting themselves at risk or causing serious mental and emotional strain in your life, you are likely in a toxic friendship.

There is no "one way fits all" for ending friendships, and not all of them end in a clean break. I do have some suggestions for ending them in ways that could make it less stressful and less daunting of a task.

If the friendship isn't too far beyond the surface, one way to end it, is to try and let the friendship simply fade. Limit your social interaction and time spent together. Catch up with her less and don't be as quick to return every phone call. Keep your business to yourself and conversations brief. The goal is that she'll get the point that you no longer wish to build upon the friendship.

When it comes to much deeper friendships though, this method is bound to end in a conversation that starts something like, "Ummmmm, what's up with you?"

In this case with your closer friends, it is my opinion that you have the conversation upfront. Sit your girl down and talk with her. Let her know exactly why you don't deem this friendship as fitting for your life anymore. Explain how her behavior has put you at risk or how you can no longer watch her put herself at risk. Let her know that she's traveling a path that you'd rather not. Let her know how you've grown and you know longer have the energy for her constant negativity or drama. Whatever the reason, just tell her. Don't leave it up to assumptions or drop subtle hints. Talk to her.

Keep in mind timing, location and tone. The goal is to end the friendship without backlash and chaos later. Be considerate of where, when and how you tell her what you tell her. If her relative just died, now may not be the best time. At her birthday soiree isn't the greatest place. Attacking her with attitude and heightened emotions isn't the way to go either. Be considerate. You don't hate her. You just don't see fit to have her in your immediate circle anymore, and you have that right to choose.

Hopefully by the end of the conversation, she will understand where you stand. If things get emotional and she attacks you, it is best to completely walk away and cut all ties and forms of communication.

Remember that you're ending the toxic friendship for the betterment of you. Stand firm in creating and keeping yourself in healthy environments. Ending friendships can be tough, but once the emotions subside, you'll feel free and can move on peacefully with life.

Don't Be Petty…. Emma's Eyes

When you initially engage in a friendship, the intent is for it to have longevity and last forever. However, as adults we know that things don't always go as planned. Some relationships are truly only for a season, and friendships are no different.

The problem most have when they come to grips with their friendship ending is they don't know how to properly end it. It's okay to realize that the friendship is toxic and neither party is benefiting or gaining anything from it. Not to say that friendships are strictly for personal gain, but in some way, shape or form, they are designed to be beneficial, even if it's just a person for you to vent to and that you can let your hair down with. When you notice that your friendship is more stressful than not, then maybe, just maybe, it's time to call it quits.

As stated before, being best friends with someone comes with a responsibility of being there for support, encouragement and a host of other things. More than likely, your friend knows your deepest and darkest secrets and you know hers. You all have probably seen each other at your lowest points, and you've allowed her into your heart and life in a way that others may not have had access. Life is unpredictable. If the scenario presents that your friendship is no longer capable of withstanding, the amicable thing to do would be to talk it out and agree to end the friendship.

That's it. That's all that it should take. Ending a friendship with someone is not, I repeat NOT, your moment or opportunity to spill all the tea, coffee and milk that was shared. Just as it takes strong, level-headed women to make a friendship work, it takes even stronger, level-headed women to end one.

Living in a social media world makes it easier for people to wreak havoc in someone's life. In 1.3 seconds, your business can be viewed by thousands of people. That's what we do not want to do. Sis, we are too grown to be playing those kind of childish games. The sooner you realize that, the better your life will be. Even though you may be hurt and you heart is broken, putting someone on blast on social media is not the way.

A mature woman knows how to take her losses and move on with life. Lashing out not only makes the person you're talking about look bad, but it makes you look even worse. If you take the petty route, your actions will then be questioned by your other friends. They can and should question your loyalty. If they are smart, they may end or lighten up on your friendship too, because you have proven to the world just how petty and child-like you can be.

If your ex-best friend resorts to the petty route, you should still refrain from retaliating. At the end of the day, you are a queen. Queens do not fraternize with peasants. Remain the adult and keep it moving. Here is a list of don'ts when ending a friendship:

Don't go to social media with your beef, if there is any.

Don't take this as an opportunity to spill the tea.

Don't bring up all the things you did to help her (because they were supposed to be done out of love).

Don't go sleeping with her exes, her current man or her future man (this is still off limits).

Don't make it long and drawn out; end the relationship and keep it moving.

You once had love for her and she had love for you. Just because you are not friends now for whatever reason, you should still have human compassion. Refrain from being messy. You never know, you may reconcile later down the road. But if you partake in petty activities out of emotion, you might permanently end a relationship that did not necessarily have to be ended.

Learn from The Cordial Queen.... TaVonna's Two Cents

If you thought that spreading rumors, gossiping, and backstabbing were only for junior high school girls, I'm sorry to have to be the one to tell you... some females never grow up or out of it.

Case in point. Your bestie Jasmine has spilled all your tea on the floor and didn't even offer you any (by the way, I don't even know a Jasmine). After you find out from multiple people that your girl is talking behind our back, you instantly demote this friend. I mean, you already know that what was said could only have come from her. She has completely shown you who she really is and how much she values your friendship.

It sucks when you have to end a friendship. Especially if it's one that you valued and the other individual did not. There is no need for there to be an all-out girl fight. You're better than that. Don't let her have the satisfaction. How about you demote Miss Chatty Kathy from bestie to acquaintance. That sounds very rushed so let's break this down.

It's best to start off by simply doing nothing. Even though you heard it through the grapevine doesn't mean you have to react to it. It was said behind your back and it probably wasn't that important anyway.

This also may be a good time to stop sharing secrets with this friend. She can no longer be trusted with your secrets. Hell, she can't be trusted with what you ordered at the coffee shop. She's going to notice that there is a different dynamic in the friendship, and that's fine. She needs to learn to keep her mouth shut. There is no need to get bent out of shape or act out of character. Yes, it sucks that someone you trusted betrayed you. She's fully aware of what she's done, so kill her with kindness.

You don't have to be her friend anymore. You don't have to meet up for drinks and spill the tea. And trust me, she's going to start to feel guilty about what she's done.

Set boundaries. If this is a person that you have to spend time with, simply be cordial. I'm Queen Cordial, y'all. I can sit in the same room as you, speak and keep it moving. It's as simple as:

HER: "Hey T!"

ME: "Hey."

HER: "How are you; how have you been?"

ME: "I'm fine, thank you."

Then, be sure to smile and start to engage in a different conversation, hunny. It's okay to speak. This lets the person know that you're the mature one. You're the bigger person. She's going to regret ever brewing the tea.

At the end of the day, this person does not pay your bills. Don't take any of it personal. You cannot control how others view you, how loyal they are, and what they may say about you. As my mother would say to me, "They were not your friend to begin with." Take that truth and embrace it.

You know, as I end this, I'm thinking to myself, *is this something the female species will ever stop doing to one another?* Maybe not.

BESTIE CODE 10: BESTIES JUST WANNA HAVE FUN

Hit the Local Scene… Emma's Eyes

Women take on many roles in life. Honestly it seems like the older we get, the more titles we add. We become wives, then mothers, cooks, cleaners, teachers, secretaries, masseuses, financial advisers and organizers… sheesh! The list never seems to end. As a woman, after countless days of multi-tasking and tending to others' needs, sometimes we just want to kick it with our girls. We want to let our hair down and have some fun. We may be getting older but we are not dead. There is nothing wrong with partying like it's 1999, as long as we are responsible enough to get all of our obligations in order before we do. Of course, make sure your spouse, children and households are in order; then go ahead and hit the scene with the ladies.

My aces and I are not really club hoppers, but we do like to go listen to music, have a drink and laugh at all the drunk people that are having the time of their lives (is that mean?). I personally like to go "snack" watching. It's kind of my favorite part of going out.

We do not necessarily have to go to a hype club to have our fun. We have two spots where we usually hang out. They serve different purposes, depending on what we're in the mood for that night. We have one local cantina that is a restaurant by day and a dance floor at night. We do not have to dress to impress, the music is well mixed and it serves our favorite drinks. It's our go-to when we just want to be chill and do a two-step.

We also have our other hangout on weekends, that serves the two of them a smorgasbord of chicken wings and serves me a smorgasbord of snacks to look at. I get to look at the bearded snacks, chocolate snacks (my favorite), vanilla snacks, king size snacks, and the occasional prune snack (men over 50). The point is, our hangouts are local, low key and it literally takes us thirty minutes to plan and meet up. It may take us seventeen hours to get ready, but we're women! Lateness is to be expected.

Having a local bar, pub, restaurant or other hangout for those random, "OMG, my day was shit and I need a drink," moments is perfect because we all have those days.

When you are selecting your hangout spot make sure it's a place where you all can dance, drink, laugh, talk and be merry. And of course, please be safe. Drink responsibly and have Uber or Lyft on speed dial if necessary.

Wherever you hang out locally, the most important rule of the night is NO BESTIE LEFT BEHIND. Travel in pairs at minimum. If you are single and you happen to leave the bar with a snack that day (don't act like random hook ups don't happen), please let your friends interrogate him, collect photos of IDs, license plate numbers, addresses and a blood sample.

And last but not least, if other women are on some drama (although we hope they are not; remember this book is about healthy women relationships). But to be honest, you can't win them all. Be prepared to let her know your Bestie is not alone and asses will get whooped if need be. I'm just saying. At the end of the day, girls just want to have fun!

Girls' Trip… Reneé's Reasoning

We've talked a lot about the tough stuff that friendship is built on. Let's not forget one of the best and most exuberant ways to build relationship. Take a trip together!

For many couples, their first couple's trip can be just as solidifying as their first time meeting the parents. In friendship, going on a trip together has all the makings of building a longer and stronger bond. So many things can happen and the possibilities are almost endless.

When you plan and take a trip with your friends, you get to see who your friends really are, if you don't already know. You'll learn who is the planner, the procrastinator, the responsible one, the irresponsible one, the party girl, the high maintenance girl, the bathroom diva, the crybaby drunk, the crazy drunk, the flirts, the late sleeper, the early riser, the motherly one, the ride-or-die, the call-911 one, the sensible one, the snacker, the foodies and everybody else I didn't have space or time to mention.

As for me personally, I like to take cruises. In my opinion, it's one of the best ways to get away since it's typically all-inclusive. Also, I love the water and I hate driving. Whatever tickles your fancy with traveling, take a trip with your girls and see how it all pans out. I promise you, it'll be an experience of a lifetime.

There are ways to go about group planning. If you're not going to hire a travel agent to handle the details, make sure you plan thoroughly and early enough so that everyone can prepare based on their day-to-day lives. Give the moms time to get babysitters lined up, the married ladies time to make arrangements with their spouses, and the working ladies to take vacation time from the job. Decide together where you'd like to go. Perhaps make it a yearly girls trip. Then get to planning.

One of the most effective ways to plan a girl's trip is to do the research on hotels, flights, activities and car rentals, and put together an all-inclusive package. Distribute the information to everyone desiring to go and then set a deadline for when everyone's funds should be given to one designated person. If funds aren't turned in by that day, that lady is on her own with making her travel plans happen. Give plenty of notice so that no one feels they didn't have adequate time to prepare financially.

You can also simply research the planned activities and local travel wherever you're going, and allow each lady to coordinate her own travel plans for arrival and departure. Just make sure that all of you are on the same page about where you're going, what time you need to be there, what you're doing once you get there, what to bring and how you're getting home.

Be realistic about spending money and, if you're traveling internationally, make sure everybody knows the exchange rates for currency. Consider starting a group text or social media thread for communication about the trip, so that everyone is in the loop about everything. This entire process along with the trip itself is a bonding experience for you gals.

Make it fun in different ways. Try things that some of you have never done before, like zip lining or a new cuisine. If it's a road trip, have each person plan a playlist and jam out to each other's music. Plan out themed fun for the trip, like formal dining night when everyone puts on their best dress for dinner. Get "bestie gear" like matching t-shirts or swimsuits. Just have fun with it, take lots and lots of pictures and make it a great and memorable experience. Here are some great ideas for girls' trips nationally and internationally.

- Cruises from the US

- European Boat Tours

- California Wine Vineyard Tours

- Los Vegas Strip

- Essence Festival Weekend

- Mardi Gras in New Orleans, LA

- Tour of New York City

- Pink Jeep Tour in Sedona, AZ

- Days in Dubai

- Bahama Mama Takeover

- Besties on South Beach in Miami, FL

- Island Getaway (Perhaps Aruba or Maui)

- Sunsets in San Diego, CA

- Besties in Bali

Bestie Sleepover… TaVonna's Two Cents

So it's the Essence Festival Weekend and it's totally not in the budget to plan a last minute Girl's Trip. That's okay, I've got one last two cents to put in. Plan an old-fashioned sleepover with your girls. You're never too old to have a sleepover. I'm talking about cute pajamas, snacks, and you can't forget special drinks.

Disclaimer: DO NOT CONSUME ALCOHOLIC BEVERAGES

UNLESS YOU ARE 21 AND OVER. Women should not drink alcoholic beverages during pregnancy because of the risk of birth defects. Consumption of alcoholic beverages impairs your ability to drive a car or operate machinery, and may cause health problems. Drink responsibly.

Okay, now that I got that out of the way, let's talk location. Hotels are very ideal of course and Air B&B may be an even better idea. And if push comes to shove, the bestie with the least amount of kids can kick her family out and host.

Don't forget to check these options as well...

• Phone a friend. Before booking online, give the hotel a call and just asked if they happen to have any deals. Please be pleasant and smile through the phone. This has gotten me a two-night stay in a 5-star hotel for an unbelievable rate.

• Did you know that airline miles are not only for flights? Use airline miles when you're making your next hotel booking.

• Check out sites that list accommodations after late cancellations. There are sites that allow you to book rooms for a reduced price.

The Bestie Code

www.roomertravel.com

www.cancelon.com

Now on to the important stuff: SNACKS! I'm talking straight junk food and not the snacks that Emma referred to. This is not the night for wine, cheese, and a fruit tray. Pizza knots, chicken wings, chips and salsa, popcorn, and, most importantly, cookies. This is not the weekend to be watching your figure.

Okay so, the room booked. Snacks are figured out. Now, on to the drinks. You can't forget about those. The great thing about a sleepover is, no one has to operate any vehicles. No designated drivers needed for those of us who like to sip.

Create signature cocktails for the night. You can find a million and one recipes on Google. Make up a drinking game and break the rules. Who cares!? The point is to have as much fun as possible. Oh, be sure to lock up each other's cell phones to ensure there is no drunk texting. You don't want to have a great night and a sucky morning all because your drunk fingers worked too hard.1

Talk about men and sex. Reminisce about your past. Laugh, joke, and cry. Whatever you do, just enjoy being in the moment with your girls.

Slumber parties aren't only for little girls. With the amount of stress and problems that grown women go through, a slumber party with your besties can be a great way to relieve stress and let loose. Relive those days when you were carefree and had nothing to worry about.

Just in case you need a few ideas, here are a few of our favorite "Girl's Night In" recipes you can try.

Pizza Knots

Ingredients:

1 can refrigerated biscuit dough

1 cup mini pepperonis

2/3 cup shredded mozzarella cheese

¼ cup of extra virgin olive oil

4 tbsp. melted butter

2 tbsp. minced garlic

2 tbsp. Chopped parsley

½ cup finely grated parmesan cheese

Marinara sauce (optional)

Instructions:

- Preheat oven to 400° and grease a 10" skillet with cooking spray or olive oil.

- Whisk together butter, olive oil, garlic, parsley, and Parmesan.

- Cut each biscuit in half and shape each half into a thin rectangle. Brush each piece with butter mixture, then sprinkle lightly with mozzarella and pepperoni. Roll and pinch the dough together to seal, then tie the dough into knots.

- Place stuffed knots in the skillet. Brush remaining butter mixture onto dough and sprinkle with more mozzarella and pepperoni.

- Bake until the cheese is melted and the biscuits are cooked through, 18 to 20 minutes. Serve warm with marinara.

Rotel Dip

Ingredients:

1lb ground london broil

1 block of Velveeta cheese

1 can of hot or mild rotel tomatoes with green chilies

1 packet of taco seasoning

Instructions:

- Brown the meat in a skillet.

- Cut the loaf of Velveeta cheese into cubes.

- Drain and add meat into a pot.

- Pour in salsa.

- Add cubes of Velveeta.

- Stir until all cheese is melted.

The Bestie Code Signature Cocktails

Know It All Punch

Ingredients:

2 1/2 cups pineapple juice

2 1/2 cups orange juice

1 cup rum

1/2 cup dark rum

1/4 cup coconut rum

1/4 cup fresh lime juice

3 tablespoons grenadine syrup

Optional: orange slice and maraschino cherry for garnish

Instructions:

- Stir all the ingredients together in a large pitcher or punch bowl.

- Serve over ice or blend with ice and enjoy!

Sweet Success Sangria

Ingredients:

1 bottle of (750ml) Roscato Rosso Dolce

¼ cup Brandy

1 cup orange juice

1 cup of sliced strawberries

½ cup blue berries

1 orange thinly sliced

1 1/2 oz can lemon-lime flavor carbonated beverage

Instructions:

- In a large glass or plastic pitcher stir together wine, orange juice, and brandy. If desired, sweeten to taste with agave nectar or sugar.

- Add fruit.

- Cover and chill until ready to serve .

- Just before serving, add carbonated beverage; stir gently. Serve over ice.

Adios Honey "I'm Done"

Ingredients:

4 oz Clear soda

1oz light rum

1 oz tequila

1 oz vodka

1.5 oz blue curacao liqueur

2 oz sweet and sour mix

Instructions:

- Pour all measured alcohol into a shaker with ice

- Shake well then strain into a tall glass

- Top off with clear soda

Enjoy and drink responsibly!

YOU KNOW YOU'RE BESTIES WHEN…

Being besties is not a title; it's a promise.

If you really want to be Best Friends Forever, you have to live by The Code. Maybe you have other codes that you and your friends live by. We'd love to hear about them. As long as you all have mutual respect, understanding and equal efforts within the friendship, you can experience longevity and good healthy interaction for years to come.

Friendship is important. Whether you have one bestie or six of them, live by The Code and do life together. Just for kicks and giggles, we've put together a list of bestie indications. If you don't have a bestie, who best fits within this list with you? Guess what girl; that's your best friend, whether you have acknowledged it or not.

You know you're besties when….

- People assume you have a tracking device on your friend.

- You can order your friend's favorite meal verbatim.

- You know your friend's list of allergies.

- Y'all look at each other from across the room and know exactly what the other is thinking.

- You can sense their emotions through text.

- You dislike majority of the same people.

- You know what happened on October 3rd.

- You can FaceTime half asleep in bonnets.

- You take naps at each other's houses.

- All of your family knows them and expects to see them on family vacations.

- You call each other's moms "mom."

- Your spouses accuse you of being lovers.

- You don't mind rocking matching outfits with her but would throw anybody else over a balcony if they bite your style.

- You feel comfortable telling her your secrets, no matter how deep they may be.

- You obsessed over :Fifty Shades of Grey" together.

- You know what kind of day she had and what the conversation will be about, simply by how long she holds the 'irl' in "Girl..." at the start of the chat.

- You instantly shoot each other a look and think the same thing when you witness some tomfoolery.

- You laugh hysterically at minor things, such as the use of silent letters.

- You share a countless number of inside jokes.

Cheers to good, healthy female friendships!

ABOUT THE AUTHORS

C. Reneé Mangum is a Business Development Strategist and digital influencer. She is a voice and advocate for empowering women in business, no matter what industry they want to thrive in. She is the creator and host of the BOSS Brunch, an annual entrepreneur's networking brunch tour for growing and sharing knowledge with aspiring and established entrepreneurs. She is also the creator of the Strictly Business Planner Book, a tool for entrepreneurs to prioritize and organize their businesses.

She, her husband and her son are Detroit natives enjoying the Phoenix sun. When she is not laughing hysterically at her bestie group text thread, she is traveling the world, running her business, spending time with her loved ones, eating chicken sushi with friends (seafood allergy) or taking long random naps on the sofa. She has been a member and leader of her sorority for seven years, fostering sisterhood and service nationwide.

TaVonna Symphony is a cancer survivor, lupus warrior, author, and advocate for women with chronic and invisible illnesses. Her personal journey has been the driving force behind her earnest desire and passion to encourage women to fearlessly navigate life unapologetically. She's a Life Navigation Specialist helping her audience navigate life around road blocks. She's the creator of the "My Chronically Essential Health Organizer" and the founder and facilitator of "The Lupie Mama and Co" support group.

Born and raised in St. Louis, she now resides in Mesa, AZ with her husband and two children. When she not planning her besties' lives or helping chronic illness patients find their way, you can find her in the sky flying to fun destinations, in a bakery buying cookies, or ordering planners on line. She has also been a member of her sorority for six years focusing on local philanthropies.

Emma Sheree is a lover of literature and all things creative. She is the founder of Eclectic Stereo, a blog showcasing her thoughts, ideas and opinions on a variety of music genres. She has worked on many creative projects, including an independent music magazine and now a book empowering women to be better supporters of one another. As a recently divorced mother of three, her life can get pretty busy but she's all for spending time with her besties.

She is a Detroit native but has resided in the desert of Phoenix, AZ, for over 4 years. In her spare time, she writes to perfect her craft, loves on her children and strives to be a great person all around. Learning to love herself one book at a time.

www.ingramcontent.com/pod-product-compliance
Lightning Source LLC
LaVergne TN
LVHW041544070426
835507LV00011B/923